Thank you for your
In the Hands of a Child
Your Premiere Lapbook Provider since
2002!!

Elements of Interior Design
HOCPP 1381
Published: December, 2010
ISBN Number: 978-1-60308-381-2

Authors: Katie Kubesh, Niki McNeil, Kimm Bellotto

For information about other products available from In the Hands of a Child
Call 1-866-426-3701 or visit our website at www.handsofachild.com

Entire contents of this Publication © 2010
In the Hands of a Child
3271 Kerlikowske Rd
Coloma, MI 49038

Bringing Laughter and Learning Together

In the Hands of a Child

From the day we first began using and creating Project Packs we fell in love with them. We knew that this type of hands-on learning experience was just the thing that was needed to make boring unit studies not only educational but fun and exciting too!

To help you get started with your Project Pack, we have included some of the most frequently asked questions we receive about our Project Packs.

What is a Project Pack?
A Project Pack contains both the activities and the lesson plans or research guide needed to complete the activities. Imagine your child not only learning about the life cycle of a butterfly, but also creating a cocoon of his or her own. Students don't just read the story, *Blueberry Sal* by Robert McCloskey- they enjoy a "blue day" complete with a recipe for blueberry pancakes, making a "blue" collage, and don't forget painting a "blue" picture!

Why is this a better way to learn? How does this help me?
Student learning improves when lessons incorporate hands-on projects or crafts. Children learn by doing. Project Packs put learning into their hands! The possibilities are endless when your student begins a lapbook with a Project Pack from In the Hands of a Child. There are no age or skill limits and any topic or subject can be worked into a Project Pack.

When you purchase a Project Pack from In the Hands of a Child, all the work is done for you-the parent/teacher, but not for the student. In addition, Project Packs are easy to store, are an instant review tool, a scrapbook, and a ready-made portfolio of all your student's studies.

How do I make a Project Pack?
A Project Pack is simply a file folder refolded into a shutter-style book. Open a file folder flat, fold each side into the middle and crease the fold neatly. There you have it!

What supplies do I need?
You need file folders, paper in different colors and weights*, your student's favorite coloring tools, tape, glue, scissors, and a stapler.

*For a more colorful and appealing Project Pack, it is suggested you print some of the reproducible graphics on colorful, multi-purpose paper. We recommend 24# weight or cardstock. **Email** sales@handsofachild.com **with your proof of purchase to receive a pdf download for easier copies.**

I have a Project Pack, NOW what?

We hope you are delighted with your new purchase, we'd like to share a few tips with you that we've found beneficial to other customers.
Here is a brief introduction to our product layout.

| Table of Contents | Guide | Core Concepts | Graphics | Folder Instructions | Sample Pictures |

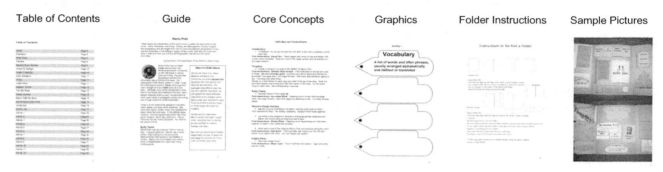

Each unit starts with a Table of Contents and is followed by a Research Guide. The Research Guide contains all of the lessons needed to complete the activities laid out in a chapter-like format. This format helps to build students' listening, reading, and comprehension skills. Included in the Research Guide is a Bibliography, which also makes a great resource for finding information for any rabbit trails you may choose to follow during your study. Related books and websites are included in the Research Guide.

Next, you will find a list of core concepts to be covered during the study, each of the concepts is represented by a graphic organizer or template. Each graphic organizer or template helps students take bite-sized pieces of information learned in the Research Guide to complete a hands-on activity to help retain that information. If you implement graded assignments in your curriculum, the list of concepts will be essential for you, the parent/teacher, to know what to test the student on. Under each concept you will find the folding instructions for each of the graphic organizers or templates. Each one has a corresponding activity number to make following along easy.

Reproducible graphics for the graphic organizers and templates follow. You will want to make a copy of each graphic for each student completing the unit. An instruction sheet for folding file folders and photos of sample lapbooks are included in the back section of each Project Pack. If you and your students are visual learners, you will find the folder instructions and sample photos quite helpful.

Project Packs from In the Hands of a Child make great stand-alone unit studies or can easily be added as a supplement to an existing curriculum. When using as a stand-alone product, we recommend completing 2 - 3 activities per session (30 - 45 minutes). Start by reading through 2 - 3 sections of the Research Guide and then complete the corresponding hands-on activities. The hands-on activities correlate to each section in the Research Guide.

Vocabulary and Timeline activities do not have to be completed in one day. Vocabulary words can be learned throughout the entire study. We recommend that your student learn a few new vocabulary words each day or learn them as they are written in the Research Guide (all words in bold are vocabulary words). We also recommend Timeline activities be completed a little each day. Choose the time periods you are going to add to your timeline as you read them in the Research Guide.

If you are working with young children or a group of children, cut out all of the graphics a day or two before beginning the lapbook and store them in a zip-top bag. It is also helpful to have all materials organized before beginning. All of our early childhood Project Packs include a full supplies list on one of the very first pages!

Your student's completed Project Pack does not have to look like the photo featured at the end of the Pack. The photo is simply a reference to help you understand the folds and the process of putting the file folder together. If you run out of room or things do not fit, add another file folder or an extension! Allow children to take an active role in designing the layout of their project so that it becomes personal for them. The personalizing of their projects aids in the reinforcement of the study.

Your students may choose to attach the various activities to their folders as each one is completed or wait until all activities are completed before attaching them to the file folder. If you choose to do the latter, simply store the activities in a zip-top bag, expandable file, or folder until you are ready to assemble them in the file folder.

Should you have any questions as you go about your study, please do not hesitate to contact us. We are here to help you bring laughter and learning together in the Hands of Your Child!!

Email sales@handsofachild.com with your proof of purchase to receive a pdf download for easier copies.

Niki
www.HandsofaChild.com

Adapting a Project Pack to Fit the Needs of Your Student

Adapting a Project or Research Pack is key to ensuring that you provide the best lesson for your student. At first glance, some might just skip over an activity because they feel it is too easy or too difficult for their student. We want you to use all the activities we provide…they are easily adaptable!

For example, if you have a PK-3 student the vocabulary activities might be difficult for him or her to complete. Here are some tips to help you adapt the activities that require your student to write:

1. Have your student dictate vocabulary words and their meanings as you write them.
2. Have your child draw a picture instead of writing.
3. You write the word or sentence first so your student can see how it is written (many of our Project Packs also include activities with dotted lines for easy copy work).
4. Practice. Practice. Practice. In the car, on a walk, in the shopping cart! Practice saying the vocabulary words and what they mean. Before you know it, your preschooler will be telling others what those words mean!
5. Contact us. We would be happy to give you ideas for adapting specific units to a grade level.

On the other hand, some of the activities may seem too easy for your student. Does your 5th grade student want to learn about butterflies, but the Project Pack seems too easy? Try it anyway; just change things up a bit to suit your student's grade level and skills. Here are some tips to help you adapt the activities to make them a little more difficult:

1. In addition to writing down vocabulary words and their meanings, ask your student to use the word in a sentence; either verbally or written.
2. Give your student one hour (or reasonable time frame) to research the topic on his or her own either online or at the library. Give your student a set of questions and see what he or she can find without your guidance.
3. Encourage your student to expand on the topic or choose a related subject to learn about.
4. Take a look at some of our preschool units…there is a lot of clipart related to each topic included. Have an older student cut these out and write a story or play about the pictures.
5. Contact us. We would be happy to give you ideas for adapting specific units to a grade level.

These are just few ways you can adapt a Project Pack to meet the needs of your student. Let your student be the judge if something is too easy or too difficult…you just might be surprised!

The Website links we have included in our guides are references we found that contain relevant information. However, the sites are not owned or maintained by In the Hands of a Child. The content may have changed or become a "dead" link. If you find the site contains inappropriate material or is no longer a relevant site, please let us know. Thank you.

Educator Notes:_____

_____

_____

_____

_____

_____

_____

_____

_____

_____

_____

_____

_____

_____

_____

_____

Table of Contents

	Vocabulary Words	Guide Reading	Complete Activities	Continue Activities
Day 1		Introduction Types of Interior Design Design Styles	2 – Types of Design 3 – Design Styles	
Day 2	function harmony budget	Design Concepts *Green Design *Budget	1 – Vocabulary 4 – Design Concepts 5 – Budget	3 – Design Styles
Day 3	audit breadth moldings	Let's Design a Room Step 1: Sketch the Room Step 2: Conduct a Room Audit	6 – Steps to Design Room 7 – Include in Sketch 8 – Sketch the Room	1 – Vocabulary 3 – Design Styles
Day 4		Step 3: Draw a Floor Plan *Why North? Step 4: Determine Furniture Layout	9 – Room Audit 10 – Floor Plan 11 – Furniture Layout Factors	3 – Design Styles
Day 5		Step 4: Determine Furniture Layout	12 – Furniture Layouts 13 – Importance of Focal Point 14 – Axis for Room	
Day 6	hue adjacent	Step 5: Lighting Step 6: Choose a Color Scheme	15 – Lighting 16 – Two Types of Lighting 17 – Color Schemes 18 – Designer Recommended Color Division	1 – Vocabulary

Schedule is continued on next page.

Have student complete vocabulary words scheduled for each day from Activity 1. Read the sections of the guide scheduled for the day and any extra books you have on the topic. Finish up each day by completing the activities scheduled for that day.

NOTE: Items marked with a * are in text-boxed areas in the guide.

Day 7	synthetic	Step 7: Choose Wall Treatment Step 8: Choose Fabrics	19 – Wall Treatments 20 – Fabric Chart	1 – Vocabulary
Day 8	cabriole veneer inlay resilient flooring	Step 9: Choose Furniture *Famous Furniture Step 10: Choose Window Treatment Step 11: Choose Flooring	21 – Questions about Furniture 22 – Window Treatment 23 – Groups of Flooring	1 – Vocabulary
Day 9		Career Opportunities Decorator or Designer?	24 – Specialized Design 25 – Decorator or Designer?	
Day 10			Extension Activities	

Related Reading

Becoming an Interior Designer: A Guide to Careers in Design by Christine M. Piotrowski

Design and Decorate Your Room by Felicity Everett and Paula Woods

How to Make Great Stuff for Your Room by Mary Wallace

Interior Design Course: Principles, Practices, and Techniques for the Aspiring Designer by Tomris Tangaz

The Nest Home Design Handbook: Simple Ways to Decorate, Organize, and Personalize Your Place by Carley Roney

Textiles by Meryl Doney

The Victorian Home by Bobbie Kalman

Bibliography

Article Dashboard. (2005-2010). *10 Fun Facts About Interior Design.* Retrieved September 2010, from Article Dashboard: http://www.articledashboard.com/Article/10-Fun-Facts-About-Interior-Design/404795

Ball, Victoria Kloss. (1995). *Opportunities in Interior Design and Decoration.* New York City: VGM Publishers.

Gittins, Jennifer. (2009, June 3). *6 Basic Interior Design Rules.* Retrieved September 2010, from Suite 101.com: http://www.suite101.com/content/6-basic-interior-design-rules-a122558

LoveToKnow Corp. (2006-2010). *Interior Decorating on a Budget.* Retrieved September 2010, from Love to Know: http://interiordesign.lovetoknow.com/Interior_Decorating_on_a_Budget

Scripps Networks, LLC. (2010). *Inside Decorating.* Retrieved September 2010, from DIY Network: http://www.diynetwork.com/decorating/index.html

Scripps Networks, LLC. (2010). *Top 10 Tips for Adding Color to Your Space.* Retrieved September 2010, from HGTV.Com: http://www.hgtv.com/decorating/top-10-tips-for-adding-color-to-your-space/index.html

The Interior Design Society. (2004-2008). *Interior Decorating- The Basics.* Retrieved September 2010, from The Creative Home: http://www.the-creative-home.com/interior-decorating.html

Activities and Instructions

Vocabulary

1. As you go through this unit, learn a few new vocabulary words each day. It is NOT necessary to learn every word included in this unit. Pick and choose the words you feel need to be learned.

Fold Instructions: *Vocab Mini Book* – Stack pages with cover on top and staple at the left edge. Write one word and definition per page.

Types of Interior Design

2. Explain the two types of interior design.

Fold Instructions: *Concept Book* – Cut on dotted line to create two flaps. Fold flaps up and write the names of one type per flap. Open flaps and write explanation inside.

Design Styles

3. Create file cards for each type of design style. You do not need to complete this activity in one sitting. Work on two or three file cards each day until you have one for each style.

Fold Instructions: *File Folder & Cards* – Fold side tabs on Templates A and B accordion style and glue to inside of the opposite template. Fold back the bottom tab on Template A and glue to the back of Template B. Glue completed file folder to lapbook. Write facts on file cards. Store completed files in folder.

Design Concepts

4. Briefly explain the three concepts of design.

Fold Instructions: *Three Door Book* – Cut on dotted lines to create three flaps. Fold flaps over and title covers with the name of one concept each. Open flaps and write explanations beneath.

Budget

5. Make a list of design tips to use when working within a budget.

Fold Instructions: *Fan Book* – Stack pages with cover on top and fasten with a brad. Write one tip per page.

Let's Design a Room!

6. List the eleven main steps for designing a room.

Fold Instructions: *Accordion Book* – Write one step per page. Keeping cover on top, fold one page back, one forward and so on. Join page sets by gluing them together at the end tabs. Glue the last (blank) page to lapbook.

Step 1: Sketch the Room

7. What important facts should be included in a sketch of a room?

Fold Instructions: *Wheel* – Write one fact per section. Cut out window section of top wheel. Place top wheel on bottom wheel and fasten with a brad. Turn wheel to view each fact.

8. Choose a room in your house and pretend you have been hired to design it. Sketch the room.

Fold Instructions: *Art Frame* – Folding is optional. You may choose to simply mount your art or fold it in fourths and attach back of last fourth to lapbook.

Step 2: Conduct a Room Audit

9. Conduct an audit of the room you have chosen to design and record your observations.

Fold Instructions: *Clipboard Book* – Use as many pages as you need to record your audit observations. Stack pages, with cover page on top and place on top of template B. Place template A on top of the stacked pages and fasten together with brads where indicated.

Step 3: Draw a Floor Plan

10. On graph paper, draw a floor plan of the room you have chosen to design. Make sure you note the location of north.

Fold Instructions: *Graph Paper* -- Folding is optional. You may choose to simply mount your graph paper or fold it in fourths and attach back of last fourth to lapbook.

Step 4: Determine the Furniture Layout

11. List and describe the four factors that an interior designer considers when determining furniture layout.

Fold Instructions: *Tab Book* – Stack pages with cover on top and so the tabs line up one after the other. Staple at the left edge.

12. Make 2-3 copies of a floor plan and give each a different furniture layout.
Fold Instructions: *Use Graph Paper from Activity 10*

13. In your own words, explain the importance of determining a focus or focal point for a room. Name four things that make good focal points for a living room or den.

Fold Instructions: *Over and Under Book* – Follow the illustrated instructions included with this activity to complete the fold.

14. Using one of the floor plans you created, establish an axis for the room.
Fold Instructions: *Use one of the floor plans you made for Activity 12.*

Step 5: Plan the Lighting

15. Why is lighting important to a room? What should be considered when determining the location of lighting?

Fold Instructions: *Two Door Book* – Cut on dotted lines to create two flaps. Fold flaps down. Write answers beneath flaps.

16. Name and describe the two types of lighting used in design.
Fold Instructions: *Up and Down Book* – Fold upper most section down, fold lower most section up, and then fold in half like a book and attach title label. Write about one type of lighting on each side of the book.

Step 6: Choose a Color Scheme
17. Describe the three main color schemes that designers use.
Fold Instructions: *Three Door Book* – Cut on dotted lines to create three flaps. Fold flaps over and write the name of the scheme on the cover and the description inside.

18. How do some designers recommend dividing colors in a room?
Fold Instructions: *Triangle Petal Book* – Keeping title to the inside of the book, write one division per section then fold one petal down on top of the next. Tuck one end of last petal under the petal next to it.

Step 7: Choose a Wall Treatment
19. Describe the five principle wall treatments most often used.
Fold Instructions: *Fan Card* – Stack pages with cover on top and fasten with a brad. Write about one treatment per page.

Step 8: Choose Fabrics
20. Create a chart showing some of the advantages and disadvantages of ten common types of fabrics used in design.
Fold Instructions: *Chart Book* – Follow the illustrated instructions included with this activity to complete the fold. Design a cover and title it "Getting a Feel for Fabrics." Fill out the chart with the 10 common fabrics you've learned about.

Step 9: Choose Furniture
21. Make a list of questions you should ask when choosing furniture.
Fold Instructions: *Blooming Wedge* – Fold back tabs on pocket and glue to lapbook. Cut wedge template on dotted line. Fold one wedge behind another until it looks like a single wedge. Store folded wedge in pocket.

Step 10: Choose Window Treatments
22. Briefly explain the relationship between window treatments and function, mood, and harmony.
Fold Instructions: *Flip Flap Book* – Fold right section over center, fold left section over center and then fold top section down and attach title label. Answer each prompt in its section.

Step 11: Choose Flooring
23. Give examples from the two groups of flooring.
Fold Instructions: *Opposite Books* – Fold each book in half so that titles remain on top. One will open upward and the other downward. Glue books to lapbook side-by-side. Answer each prompt under its flap.

Career Opportunities

24. What are four areas that would fall under specialized design?

Fold Instructions: *Diamond Book* -- Follow the illustrated instructions included with this activity to complete the fold. Number the flap covers 1 – 4 then open flaps and write about one area under each one.

25. What is the difference between an interior decorator and an interior designer?

Fold Instructions: *Slit Tab Book* – Cut a slit on the dotted line. Fold book in half and slide tab into slit. Open book and write answer inside.

EXTENSION ACTIVITIES

- Have a friend or family member pretend she is a new client of yours. She has hired you to redesign a room in her house (*not* the kitchen or bathroom!). Talk to her about what the room will be used for and any ideas she has for the room – think function, mood, and harmony. Discuss colors schemes and your client's personal style. Once you have a good idea of what the client is looking for, tell her to give you a budget to work within, and then go to different types of stores or search online to find things you would choose for the redesign. For example, go to a fabric store, a paint store, a lighting store, a furniture store, etc. Keep a list of the items you would choose for the room along with their prices in order to stay on budget. Collect fabric color swatches, flooring samples, paint or wallpaper samples, and pictures of furniture to present with a floor plan and sketches to your client.

- Choose one of the following topics for further research:
  - ➢ design styles
  - ➢ furniture styles
  - ➢ fabrics
  - ➢ flooring materials
  - ➢ ceiling materials

- Research and write a report on the history of interior design.

- Design an entire home for a pretend family. Write a composition describing the family that lives in the home, including number of people, children, ages, genders, income, hobbies and in-home activities, pets, and any other relevant information.

Creating a Lapbook Base

Basic Lapbook Base

- Open a file folder and lay it flat.
- Fold both right and left edges toward the center so they meet and close like a pair of shutters.
- Crease firmly.

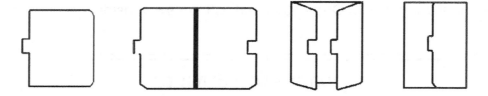

Base with Single or Double Extensions

- Complete the basic lapbook base.
- Open base and lay flat.
- Cut another folder in half or use a sheet of cardstock for the extension.
- Lay the extension in the center of folder at either the top or bottom. (You may add two extensions if need be; one at the top and one at the bottom).
- Attach to base with clear packing tape.

Single Extension   Double Extension

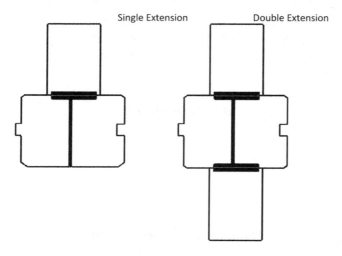

Double Folder Base

- Make two base folders.
- Open them and lay them side by side with outer flaps pointing straight up, not flat.
- Where the two flaps meet glue them together.
- Fold center flap to one side, fold both shutters in and close folders like a book.

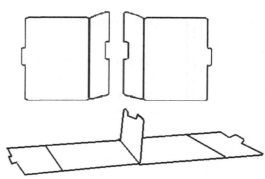

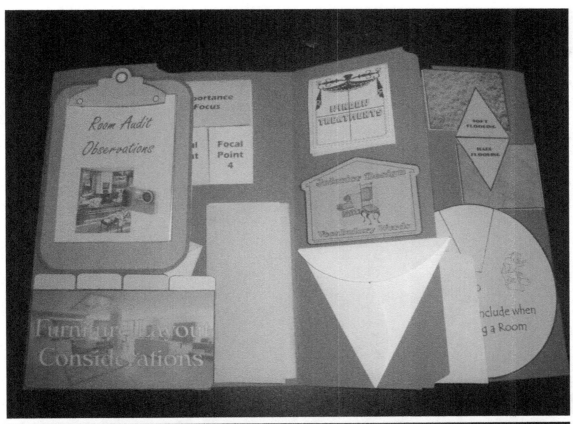

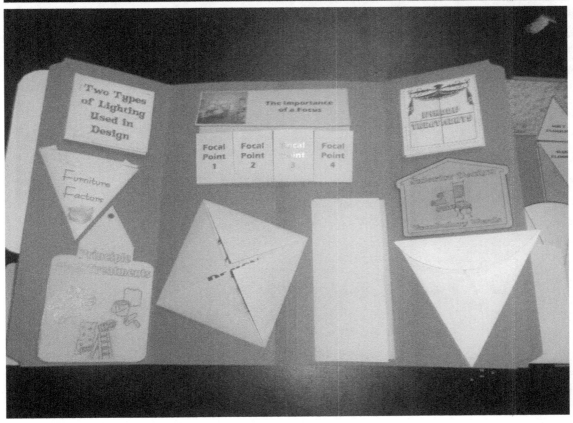

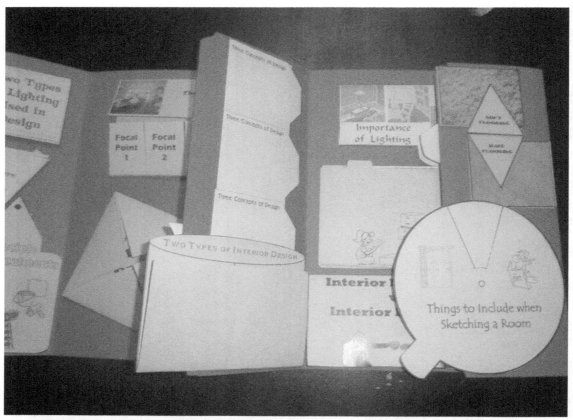

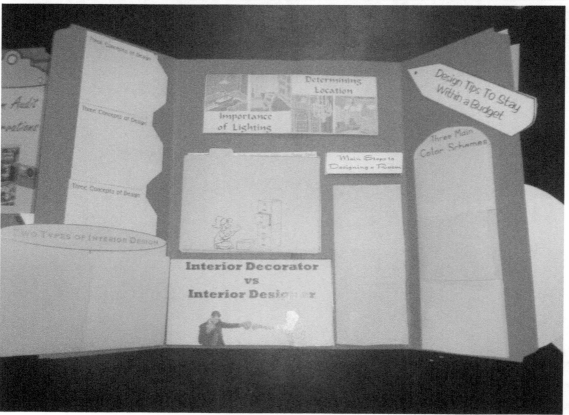

Elements of Interior Design

 What do you think about when you hear the words "interior design"? Colors, fabrics, furniture, styles, and textures are all words that may come to mind. As you read on, you will also begin to think of the words *function*, *mood*, and *harmony*. In interior design, all of these factors are carefully selected to create a specific look for each individual room in a home, office, or other environment.

Types of Interior Design

There are two types of interior design: decorative and structural. Structural design relates to size and shape of an object. It is based on simplicity, proper use of materials, proportion, and appropriateness for the way the room will be used. Decorative design is based more on embellishment. While appropriateness to the basic structure is still required, more emphasis is put on the details with additions to structural elements through carved pieces, upholstering, and ornamentation, and decorative pieces with color, line, and texture.

Design Styles

There are many different design styles, including

- Art Deco: Art deco, popular in the 1920s and 1930s, is a streamlined, geometric style. Furnishings in this style consist of rounded fronts, sleek lines, glass accessories, and chrome hardware.

- Colonial: The colonial style, based on American furniture designs of the 1600s through the American Revolution, consists of wood, spindle designs, needlepoint and embroidery samplers, and simple craftsmanship.

- Contemporary: Contemporary design includes a wide range of styles from the late 20th century, such as rounded soft lines, neutral elements, and a focus on form, line, and shape.

- Country: Styles with a country influence consist of muted colors, milk-paint finishes, vintage fabrics, and rustic or primitive furnishings.

- Eclectic: Eclectic style is a variety of different styles and periods that are tied together with color, shape, and texture.

- French Provincial: French provincial, also called French country, is a rustic version of the formal French designs of the 1600s and 1700s. This style consists of furnishings left in their natural state, caning instead of upholstery, and natural colors such as terra cotta and stone.

- <u>Mission</u>: Mission style, influenced by the American arts and crafts movement, consists of darkly finished heavy furniture with straight and simple lines.

- <u>Traditional</u>: Traditional design style borrows from the style of England and France during the 18th and 19th centuries. It is calm, orderly, and predictable. Popular furnishings from this style include tailored looks, fringe embellishments, crystal, and silver.

- <u>Victorian</u>: Victorian style, named after England's Queen Victoria, was very popular in the late 1800s. Furnishings consist of elaborately carved mahogany, walnut, and rosewood. Fabrics are bold and colors are strong and are usually embellished with fringe or other trimmings.

Design Concepts

When designing a room, the concepts of room **function**, mood, and **harmony** must be considered at each step of the design process.

- <u>Room function</u>: A designer's job is to find out what the function of a room will be: how the room will be used, and who will be using it. A room could be the most beautifully designed space in the world, but if it cannot fulfill all the functions required of that room, the design has failed. For example, one of the main functions of a dining room is eating. When a designer is creating a dining room, he must make sure the room is a convenient place in which to eat. An ideal room is one that provides the most functionality for the owner's lifestyle.

- <u>Mood</u>: Is the client looking for a sleek, modern space or something more casual and warm? A designer must consider the mood a client is trying to express in the room being designed and then use color schemes, furniture, flooring, lighting, and window treatments that are consistent with that mood.

Green Design

A fairly new style in interior design is Green Design. As people have become more conscious about how they use the planet's resources, they are incorporating green ideas into designs.

Some of the ways that we can incorporate "green" into interior design is by creating designs that are energy efficient such as installing compact fluorescent lamps that use less energy, replacing existing appliances with energy efficient appliances, installing solar panels, and regulating interior temperatures with window treatments.

- <u>Harmony</u>: Another guideline that designers must consider is harmony, making sure that all the elements in a room work together to provide function and mood for the client. To ensure harmony, all elements of a design should have a compatible color scheme, a consistent scale, and matching quality. For example, if a designer furnishes a room with high-end leather furniture, she will not want to add an inexpensive plastic coffee table to the design.

Pay close attention to the three design concepts: function, mood, and harmony...you will see them again, and again, and again!

Let's Design a Room!

One of the best ways to learn the concepts of interior design is to design a room. The main steps to designing a room are:

1. Sketch the room
2. Conduct a room **audit**
3. Draw a floor plan
4. Determine the furniture layout
5. Plan the lighting
6. Choose a color scheme
7. Choose a wall treatment or treatments
8. Choose fabrics
9. Choose furniture
10. Choose window treatments
11. Choose flooring

Budget

In addition to the three main design concepts, most designers usually have to work within a budget.

Some great design tips when working within a budget are:

- Prioritize which rooms, projects, and elements are the most important.

- Assess the room for existing furnishings and accessories that can be used in the new design.

- Improve, repaint or reinvent uses for existing items instead of replacing them.

- Cover imperfections on items instead of replacing them.

- Use mirrors to create light and space.

- Buy unfinished products and finish them yourself.

- Buy secondhand or recycled products.

Step 1: Sketch the Room

The first step in designing a room is to create a rough sketch of it. When sketching the room, make sure you include important factors such as:

- Length of the room
- Ceiling height
- **Breadth** of the room
- Height of **moldings**
- Dimensions of doors and windows
- Distance between windows and doors from the corners and from the ceiling and floor
- Measure any room features such as air conditioner units, built-ins, fireplaces, etc.
- Location of electrical outlets and switches
- Location of lighting fixtures

Step 2: Conduct a Room Audit

After you have sketched the room and its important features, you will need to audit the condition of the room and record your observations. This will help you determine what needs to be repaired or replaced before you begin decorating. It is helpful to take photographs of every angle of the room so you will have a reference during the rest of the design process.

Step 3: Draw a Floor Plan

The best tool for this step is graph paper. When you draw your floor plan, simply redraw your rough sketch to scale on graph paper. Many designers use a scale of 1/4 inch = 1 foot or ½ inch = 1 foot. Your floor plan should include:

- Location of doors and windows
- Location of North

7'-6" MIN.

7'-6"

· K I T C H E N ·

D I N E T T E

Why North?

N

Why should your floor plan show where North lies? Knowing where North is helps a designer determine where the sun will rise in relation to the room's windows, how much sun light the room will have, how the sun can be used to warm the room each morning, and whether the room needs to be shaded from the sun.

Step 4: Determine the Furniture Layout
You have completed a rough sketch and a floor plan, now it's time to determine where the furniture will go in the room. A good interior designer considers four factors when determining the layout of furniture in a room.

> Make several copies of your floor plan and then draw different furniture layouts before deciding which one you or your client likes best.

1. Balance Lines: To determine the balance lines of the room, you will need to divide the room into four quadrants. Draw two pencil lines across the floor plan to divide the room in half length wise and breadth wise. To keep the room balanced, you will need to have an equal weight of furniture in each quadrant. Your four quadrants do not have to be mirror images of each other; you just want to create a visual balance of furniture.

2. Traffic Patterns: Determine where the traffic patterns will be and mark them on the floor plan to remind you not to put furniture in these places. Many designers recommend leaving 36 inches clear in front of each door opening for the swing of the door and 12 inches clear in front of windows for easy access.

3. Focus: Now is the time to determine what the focus or focal point of the room will be. For example, focal points to consider for a living room or den include fireplaces, home theaters, artwork, and bay windows. Once you have determined the focus of the room, your design will revolve around it.

4. Axis: To establish an axis for the room, draw (to scale) the wall that contains the room's focal point and the wall opposite of the focus. Next, draw a line up the middle of the wall from floor to ceiling through the focus, across the ceiling, and down the opposite wall to the floor. This will help you balance the focus from floor to ceiling. For example, if your focus is a home theater, you will need to put something on the opposite wall of equal visual weight along the axis line.

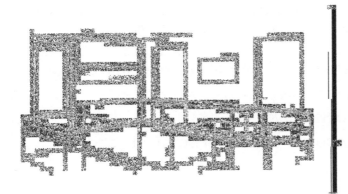
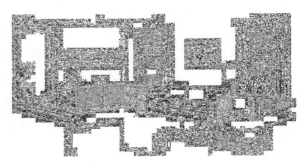

Step 5: Plan the Lighting

Lighting is a very important element in a room. It helps to make the room functional and it creates a mood. When determining the location of lighting, make sure to pay attention to where the electrical outlets are situated!

There are two types of lighting you must provide in a room:

1. <u>Task lighting</u> allows people who use the room to complete tasks such as reading, crafts, and hobbies.

2. <u>Ambient lighting</u> gives sufficient light so people can see where they are going in the room.

Designers say, "Light the objects in a room, not the room!"

Step 6: Choose a Color Scheme

You can build your color scheme around one color or around two or more colors. Once you have decided on a color scheme you can pick out paint colors, fabric colors, and window treatments that fit the scheme. Designers usually use three main color schemes:

> The name of a specific color is the hue. Warm hues are red, orange, and yellow; cool hues are blue, green, and violet; neutral hues are white, black, and brown.

1. <u>Adjacent Schemes</u>: When colors that are used are **adjacent** to each other on the color wheel, the design is an adjacent color scheme. Examples of adjacent colors are yellow and green, yellow and orange, orange and red, red and purple, purple and blue, and blue and green.

2. <u>Complementary Schemes</u>: When colors that are used are opposite each other on the color wheel, the design is a complementary color scheme. Examples of complementary colors are yellow and purple, green and red, and blue and orange.

3. <u>Monochromatic Schemes</u>: When a major color is the predominant *and* the accent color, the design is a monochromatic color scheme.

> Some designers advise dividing colors for a room into three percentages:
> - 60% of a dominant color – walls
> - 30% of a secondary color – window treatments and upholstery
> - 10% of an accent color – accessories

Step 7: Choose a Wall Treatment

You have chosen your color scheme, now how will you use it on the walls? Determining wall treatments depends, like everything else in your design, on the three design concepts: function, mood, and harmony.

- Function: Consider the function of the room when determining the wall covering. High traffic areas will need a covering that resists scuffmarks, fingerprints, and dirt such as tiles or washable paint.

- Mood: The wall treatment will greatly influence the mood of the room. For example, if you are trying to establish a bright, cheerful mood, you won't want to choose a dull or muted color for the walls.

- Harmony: Create balance in the room by harmonizing the wall treatment with the furniture, artwork, and other features in the room. If you are planning to place floral patterned furniture in the room, you may want to either repeat the pattern on the walls or go for a solid color.

Use the design concepts above to help you determine which wall treatment works best for your design. There are five principle wall treatments most often used:

1. Fabric: Fabric gives added texture to a wall and can produce a rich, warm mood to a room.

2. Mirrors: Mirror treatments allow the designer to make a room look bigger and to increase the amount of light.

3. Natural: Natural materials such as brick, stone, tile, or wood create an earthy mood for the room. Others, such as shells, bamboo, and rattan, can make a room feel light and airy.

4. Paint: Paint is usually the least expensive and most common wall treatment. It is also the most versatile.

5. Wallpaper: Wallpaper, which is usually a plastic or plastic coated paper, is available in solid colors, patterns, and even full wall murals.

Step 8: Choose Fabrics

Fabric decisions should be based on the design concepts function, mood, and harmony.

- Function: To determine which fabric meets the function, consider if the cost fits the budget of the room and if the fabric needs to be dirt resistant, durable, or sun resistant.

- Mood: To determine which fabric meets the mood of a design, inspect the fabric for good texture, color, and feel for the mood you want to create in the room.

- Harmony: The fabric you choose must be harmonious with other fabrics you will be using as well as the design of the entire room. Patterns, colors, and qualities of the fabrics you choose should be similar.

There are two main types of fabric fibers: natural fabric fibers and **synthetic** fabric fibers. Natural fabric fibers include cotton, wool, linen, and silk. Synthetic fabric fibers include acrylic, glass, nylon, polyester, and rayon. Fabrics may be made of one type of fiber or a combination or fibers. Each has advantages and disadvantages; see the chart below for some fundamentals of fabrics commonly used in design.

Fabric Type	Advantages	Disadvantages
Acrylic fabric	Strong, durable, resists insects, mildew and weathering; wrinkle resistant	Generates static electricity, does not absorb moisture, can be uncomfortable
Cotton	Tough material, withstands wear, breathes well, dries quickly	Has a tendency to wrinkle
Glass fabric	Flame resistant, resists insects, mildew, sun damage, and water	Has a tendency to crack
Hemp	Extremely strong and durable, hypo-allergenic, breathes well, resists mildew, absorbs moisture	Wrinkles easily, may be scratchy unless blended with a softer fiber, is not colorfast
Linen	Durable, retains its shape, resists bacteria, dirt, and stains; is naturally lint-free	Wrinkles easily, not as durable as cotton and wool, hard to dye
Nylon	Strongest of all fabrics, easy to dye, repels mildew and moths, washable, dries quickly	Shiny appearance, slippery, flammable, easily damaged by the sun
Polyester	Flame resistant, strong, resists dirt, mildew, and moths; washable	Does not dye well, fades in sunlight
Rayon	Inexpensive alternative to silk, easy to dye	Not very strong, subject to mildew, rots in sunlight
Silk	Luxurious, soft, strong, dyes beautifully	Hard to clean, fades easily
Wool	Tough, durable, soft, luxurious, dyes easily	Delicate, expensive

Step 9: Choose Furniture

There are so many options available in furniture. Consider these factors when choosing furniture:

- Does the cost meet the budget?
- Will the piece function in the room?
- What overall style do you want?
- Does it match the mood and style of the design?
- Is the piece harmonious with other pieces in the room?
- Is the piece the right size for the space?

Some furniture styles to choose from include:

- <u>Mediterranean Styles</u> include Italian Renaissance (1400s) and Spanish style (1500s). It is the oldest style that is still used today. Both Italian Renaissance and Spanish styles are heavy, solid, and usually ornately carved.

- <u>French Styles</u> include Louis XIV (1643-1715), Regence (1700-1730), Louis XV (1370-1775), Louis XVI (1775-1789), Directoire (1790-1804), and Empire (1804-1831).

- <u>English Styles</u> include Tudor, also called Jacobean (end of the 16th century to the 17th century), William and Mary (1689-1702), Queen Anne (1702-1714), Early Georgian (1714-1760), Late Georgian (1760-1811), Regency (1810-1837), and Victorian (1837-1901).

- <u>Early American Styles</u> include Federal and American Empire styles. Before the Civil War, American furniture styles were influenced by the Greek revival style; after the Civil War, designs were influenced by the Victorian era.

- <u>Arts and Craft Style</u>, also called Mission style, is based on the arts and crafts movement of 1880 to 1910. This style of furniture has a simple, utilitarian design.

- <u>20th Century Styles</u> includes furniture made from wood, metal, glass, and plastic. Major 20th Century styles are Art Nouveau, Art Deco, Bauhaus, and Post Modernism.

Famous Furniture

<u>Chippendale (1750-1790):</u> Thomas Chippendale was a British designer and cabinet maker. His work was greatly influenced by French, Chinese, and Gothic styles. Characteristics of Chippendale furniture include ball-and-claw foot, cabriole legs, and scroll top pieces.

<u>Hepplewhite (1765-1800):</u> George Hepplewhite style furniture has a delicate appearance with characteristics such as tapered legs, and contrasting **veneers** and inlays.

<u>Duncan Phyfe (1795-1848):</u> Duncan Phyfe was an American cabinetmaker. This style of furniture is characterized by carved legs and neoclassic motifs.

Step 10: Choose Window Treatments

Window treatments include curtains, colored glass, roller shades, roll up blinds, pull up blinds, Venetian blinds, vertical blinds, cornices, valances, swags, louvered shutters, and fabric shutters.

What factors do you think you need to consider when choosing window treatments? If you guessed function, mood, and harmony, you are correct!

- Function: Window treatments not only need to make the room look appealing, they must function the way they are needed to; window treatments are often used to provide privacy, control sunlight, control temperature, and control sound.

- Mood: The window treatments you select must fit the mood you are trying to create with the rest of the design. For example, if you are designing a warm, comfortable, earthy mood, you will want to select a window treatment such as bamboo or other natural materials to match that mood - not neon green plastic mini blinds!

- Harmony: Just like other design options, the window treatments should be harmonious with the rest of the design. Consider the quality and scale of the window treatment compared to the rest of the elements you are placing in the room.

Materials Used for Window Treatments

Another important factor to consider when choosing window treatments is the material. Different materials used for window treatments include aluminum, wood, fabric, faux wood, and plastic.

Aluminum, wood, faux wood, and plastic are easy to clean and range from simple to elegant.

Fabric window treatments can require more effort to put up and take down, and must be washed periodically.

Step 11: Choose Flooring

Flooring can be one of the most expensive treatments you add to a room, so cost and budget are huge factors. Since changing an existing floor is the most expensive option, it may fit the budget better if you simply cover or uncover the existing floor treatment.

You guessed it...choosing just the right flooring depends on function, mood, and harmony!

- Function: What is the main function of flooring? People walk on it! Therefore, the flooring you choose should be durable and stain resistant. In addition, the flooring must match the function of the particular room. For example, in the bathroom, you want to choose flooring that is not slippery.

- Mood: How do you set a mood with flooring? The type of materials used for flooring can play an important role in the mood of a room. For instance, marble flooring contributes to a formal mood, while wood flooring gives a more casual feel.

- Harmony: Scale is important when choosing flooring for a room. If you are designing a large room, you can feel free to choose bolder patterns and colors than you usually can in a smaller room. You can also add floor coverings such as area rugs to make a large area seem smaller.

Flooring can be divided into two groups: hard and soft.

Hard flooring treatments include wood, stone, tile, and resilient flooring.

Soft flooring treatments include carpeting and rugs.

Career Opportunities

Interior design professionals usually choose from three main career paths:

1. Commercial Design: Commercial design includes corporate offices, entertainment facilities, executive offices, healthcare facilities, hospitality facilities, retail facilities, transportation facilities, and other public or commercial venues.

2. Residential Design: Residential design includes bathroom and kitchen design, historical restoration, home renovations, model homes, and other types of renovations.

3. Specialized Design: Specialized design can vary widely. Some types of specialized design include:

> product design or product representation
> a specific focus on certain design elements such as lighting, kitchen and bath, or closet designs
> an exclusive type of client such as geriatric facilities
> a particular design style such ergonomic or environmental (green) design

Decorator or Designer?

The terms "decorator" and "designer" may seem interchangeable; however, in the interior design profession, they are two separate professions.

- <u>Interior Decorator</u>: An interior decorator is a person who applies the finishing touches to a room or design such as the wall coverings, fabric, furnishings, and accessories. There are certification and continuing education courses for interior decorating, but certification is not required to be an interior decorator.

- <u>Interior Designer</u>: An interior designer is responsible for researching the function, mood, and harmony of a space and using specialized knowledge to plan, prepare, and design the space to fit the health, safety, and wellbeing of the client. Interior designers must have a working knowledge of color theory, space planning, building codes, and plumbing and mechanical basics. This profession requires a degree from an accredited institution and a license.

Vocabulary

Adjacent: lying next to or adjoining; having a common border

Audit: a methodical examination and review

Breadth: distance from side to side

Budget: the amount of money available or designated for a certain period or purpose

Cabriole: a curving furniture leg tapering into a decorative foot

Function: the purpose or role that an object fulfills or is suited for

Harmony: a pleasant or organized relation among the parts of something

Hue: a particular shade of a color

Inlay: pieces of material set into a surface to form an ornamental design or decoration

Moldings: a strip of wood, stone, or other material used to frame or finish a door, window, or wall

Resilient flooring: floor treatment made from thin sheets of man made products like vinyl or linoleum.

Synthetic: a substance made by a chemical process and not of natural origin

Veneer: a very thin layer of fine wood that is bonded to a cheaper material to form a more attractive surface

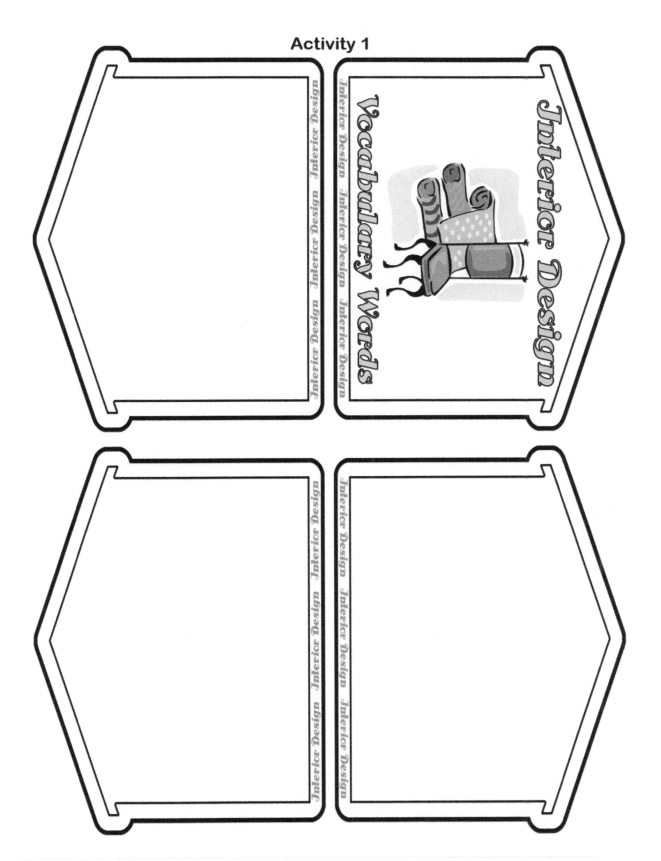

Interior Design

Vocabulary Words

Interior Design

Activity 1

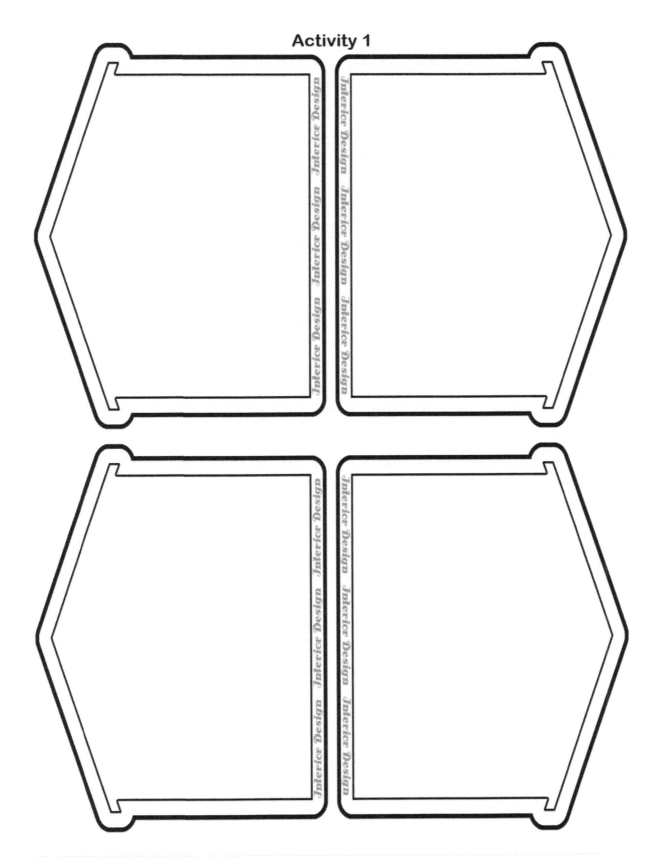

Activity 1

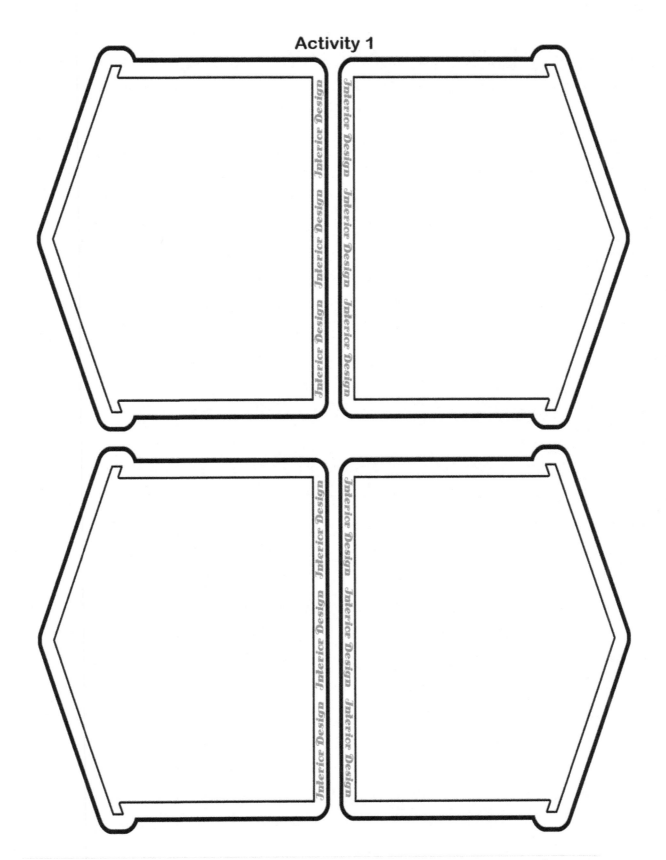

Activity 2

TWO TYPES OF INTERIOR DESIGN

Activity 3

Template A

Template B

Activity 3

_____

_____

_____

_____

_____

_____

_____

_____

_____

_____

_____

_____

_____

_____

Activity 3

Design Styles ✦ *Design Styles* ✦ *Design Styles* ✦ *Design Styles*

Design Styles ✦ *Design Styles* ✦ *Design Styles* ✦ *Design Styles*

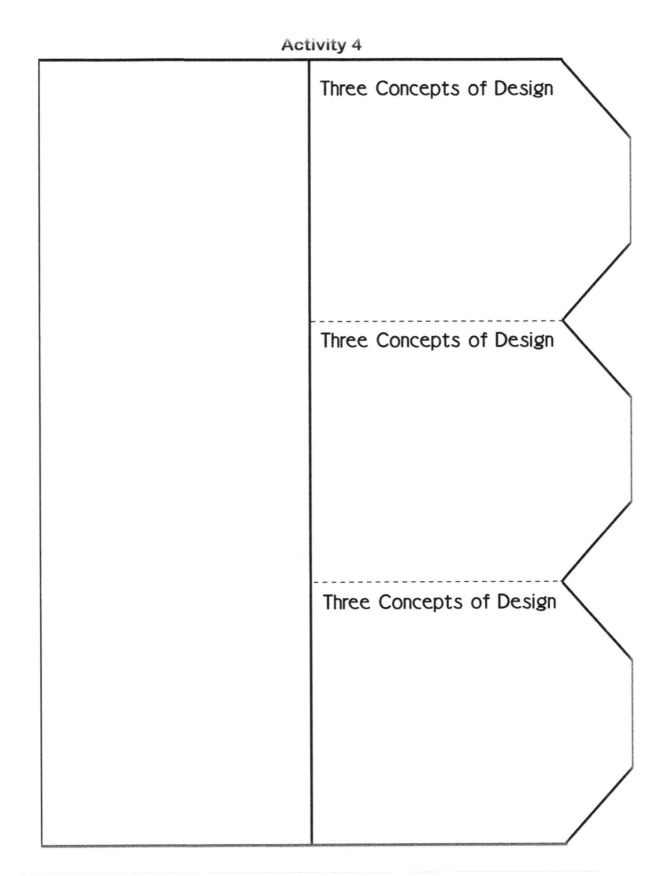

Three Concepts of Design

Three Concepts of Design

Three Concepts of Design

Design Tips To Stay Within a Budget

Activity 5

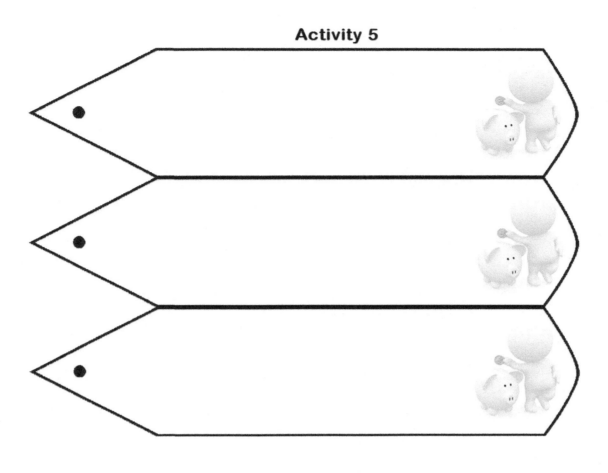

Main Steps to Designing a Room

Things to Include when
Sketching a Room

Activity 7

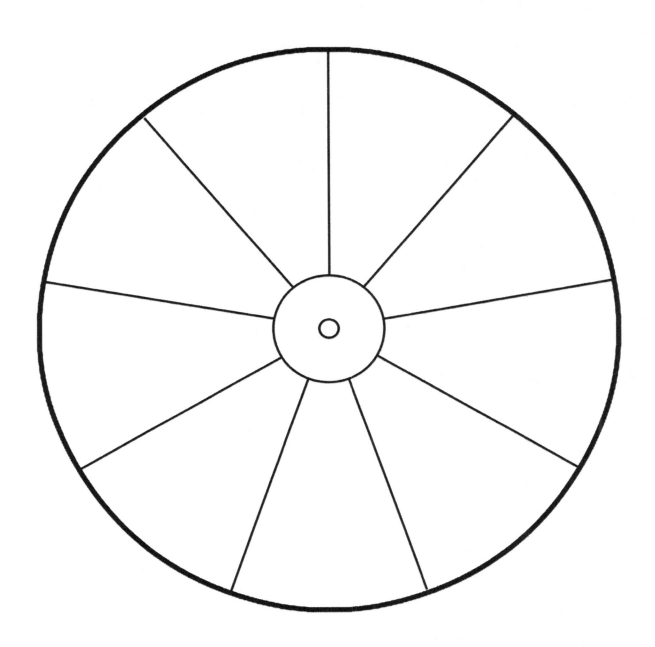

Sketch of
_____

Activity 9

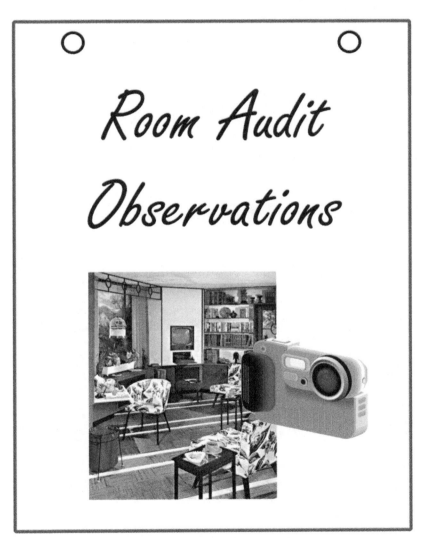

Room Audit Observations

Template A

Activity 9

Room Audit

Template B

Room Audit

Room Audit

Room Audit

Room Audit

Activity 10

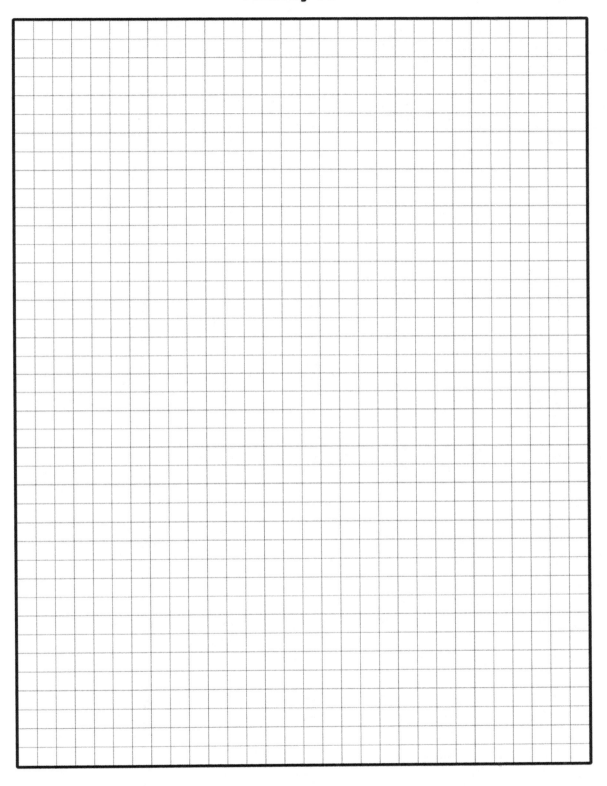

Activity 11

Furniture Layout   Furniture Layout   Furniture Layout

Activity 11

Furniture Layout   Furniture Layout   Furniture Layout

Furniture Layout   Furniture Layout   Furniture Layout

Activity 11

Furniture Layout   Furniture Layout   Furniture Layout

Activity 13

Over and Under Book

Your template may have more or fewer flaps.

Title	Title	Title

Title

Template looks like this before it's folded.

Title

Title	Title	Title

Template looks like this after it's folded.

Activity 13

Focal Point 1	Focal Point 2	Focal Point 3	Focal Point 4

The Importance of a Focus

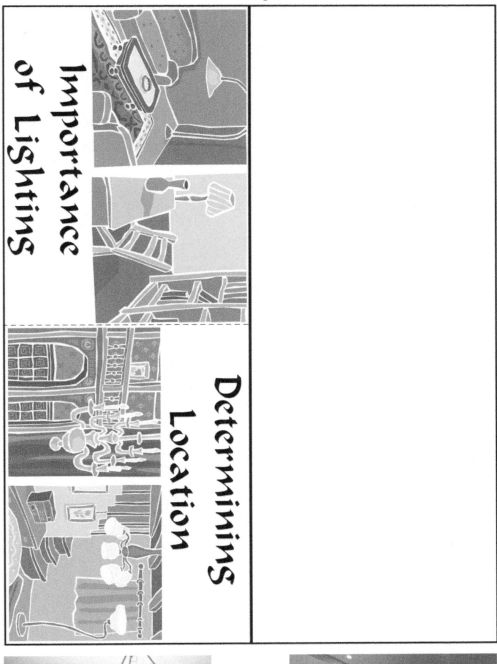

Importance of Lighting

Determining Location

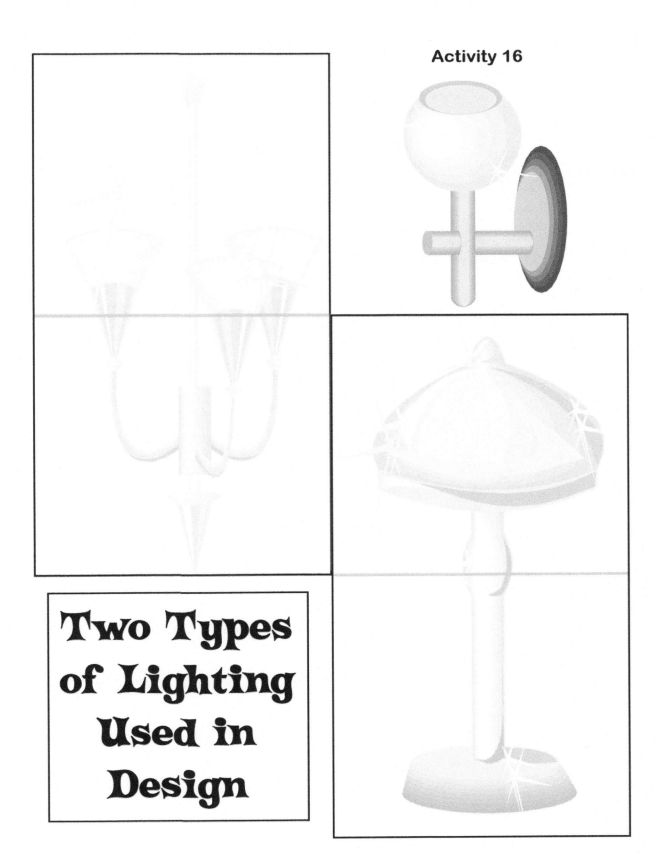

Two Types
of Lighting
Used in
Design

Activity 17

Three Main
Color Schemes

Division of Colors for a Room Design

Principle
Wall Treatments

Wall Treatments

Wall Treatments

Activity 19

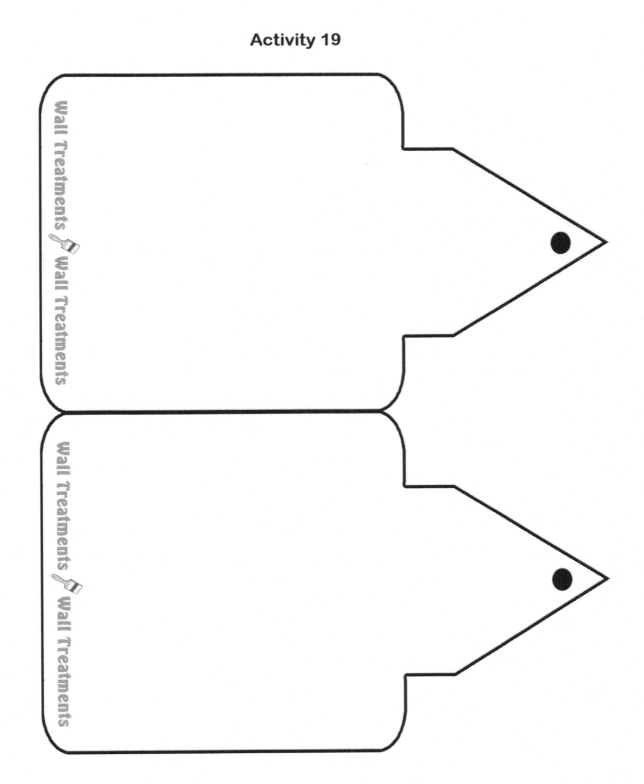

Wall Treatments Wall Treatments

Wall Treatments Wall Treatments

Activity 19

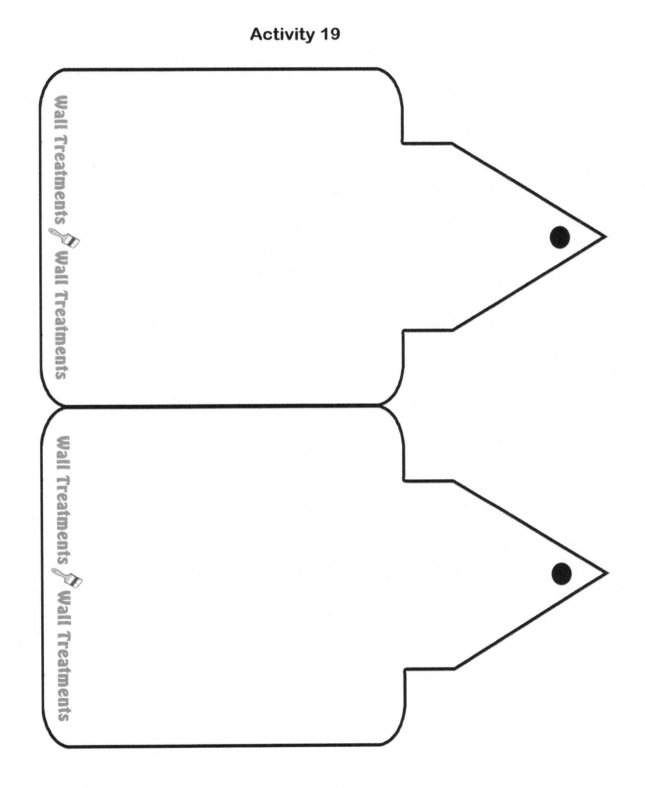

Wall Treatments Wall Treatments

Wall Treatments Wall Treatments

Activity 19

Wall Treatments

Wall Treatments

Activity 20

Chart Folding Instructions

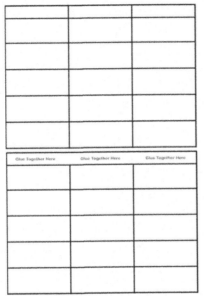

Glue upper section to lower section where indicated

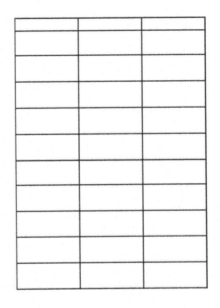

Chart now looks like this

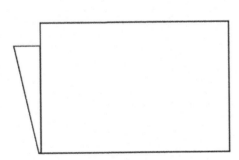

Fold in half from bottom

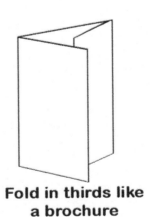

Fold in thirds like a brochure

Activity 20

Fabric Type	Advantages	Disadvantages

Glue Together Here

Glue Together Here

Glue Together Here

Activity 21

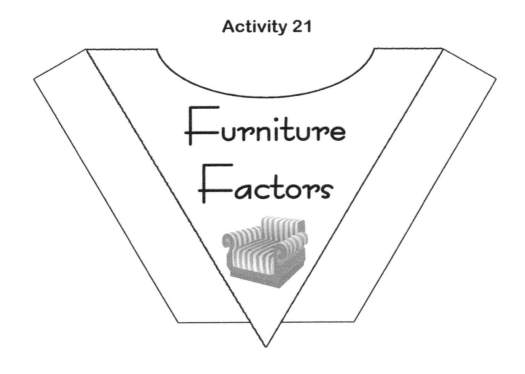

Activity 21

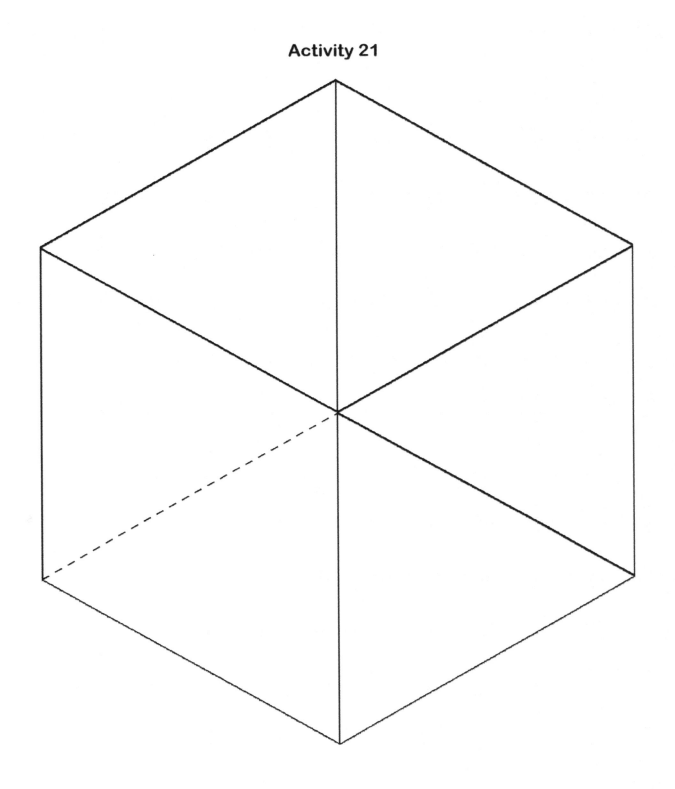

Activity 22

HARMONY

MOOD

FUNCTION

WINDOW TREATMENTS

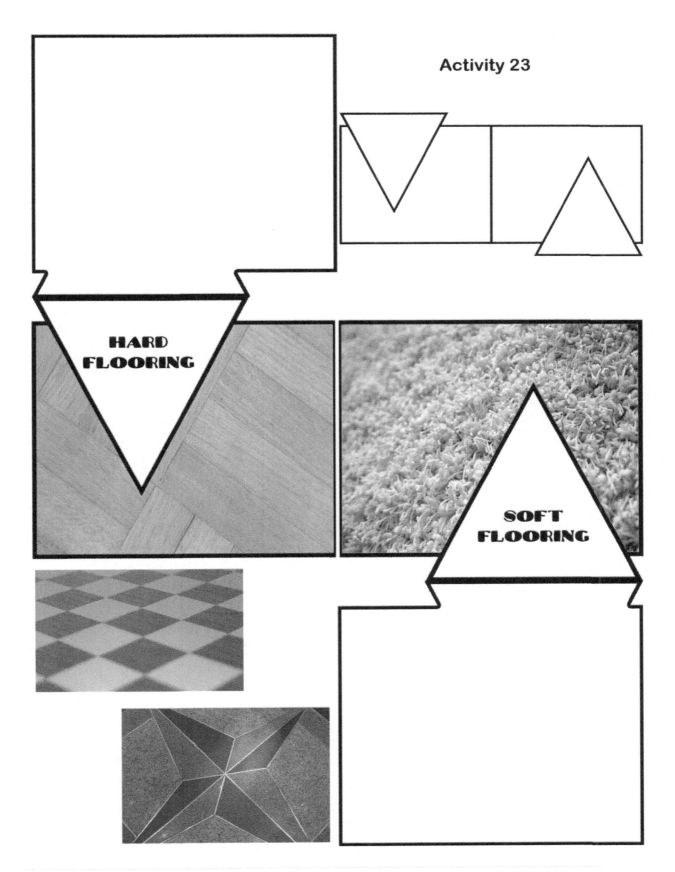

Activity 23

HARD FLOORING

SOFT FLOORING

Activity 24

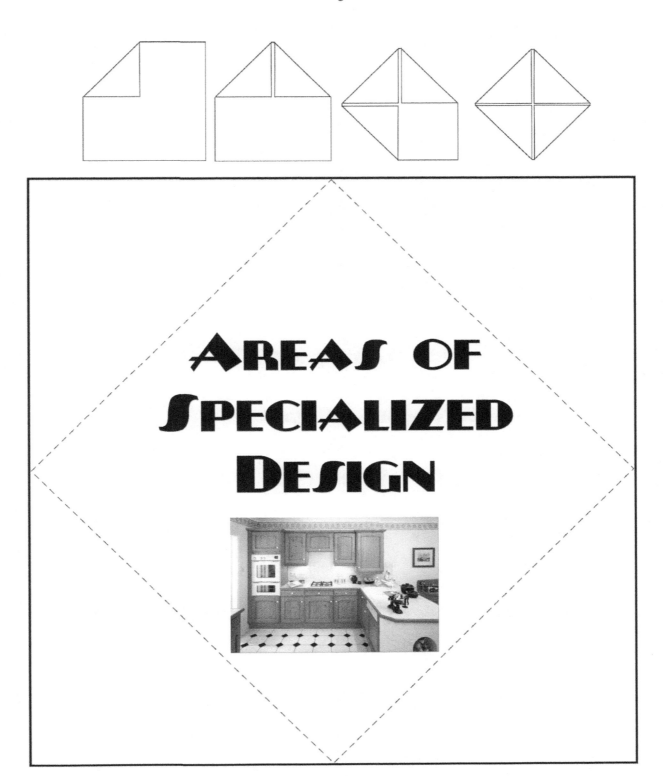

AREAS OF SPECIALIZED DESIGN

- -

Interior Decorator
vs
Interior Designer

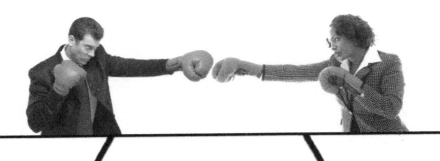

Answer Key

Activity 1: Vocabulary

1. Vocabulary: As you go through this unit learn a few new vocabulary words each day.

Answer:

See Page 32

Activity 2: Types of Interior Design

Explain the two types of interior design.

Answer:

- Structural design relates to size and shape of an object. It is based on simplicity, proper use of materials, proportion, and appropriateness for the way the room will be used.
- Decorative design is based more on embellishment. While appropriateness to the basic structure is still required, more emphasis is put on the details with additions to structural elements through carved pieces, upholstering, and ornamentation, and decorative pieces with color, line, and texture.

Activity 3: Design Styles

Create file cards for each type of design style. You do not need to complete this activity in one sitting. Work on two or three file cards each day until you have one for each style.

Answer:

- Art Deco: Art deco, popular in the 1920s and 1930s, is a streamlined, geometric style. Furnishings in this style consist of rounded fronts, sleek lines, glass accessories, and chrome hardware.
- Colonial: The colonial style, based on American furniture designs of the 1600s through the American Revolution, consists of wood, spindle designs, needlepoint and embroidery samplers, and simple craftsmanship.
- Contemporary: Contemporary design includes a wide range of styles from the late 20th century, such as rounded soft lines, neutral elements, and a focus on form, line, and shape.
- Country: Styles with a country influence consist of muted colors, milk-paint finishes, vintage fabrics, and rustic or primitive furnishings.
- Eclectic: Eclectic style is a variety of different styles and periods that are tied together with color, shape, and texture.
- French Provincial: French provincial, also called French country, is a rustic version of the formal French designs of the 1600s and 1700s. This style consists of furnishings left in their natural state, caning instead of upholstery, and natural colors such as terra cotta and stone.

- Mission: Mission style, influenced by the American arts and crafts movement, consists of darkly finished heavy furniture with straight and simple lines.
- Traditional: Traditional design style borrows from the style of England and France during the 18th and 19th centuries. It is calm, orderly, and predictable. Popular furnishings from this style include tailored looks, fringe embellishments, crystal, and silver.
- Victorian: Victorian style, named after England's Queen Victoria, was very popular in the late 1800s. Furnishings consist of elaborately carved mahogany, walnut, and rosewood. Fabrics are bold and colors are strong and are usually embellished with fringe or other trimmings.

Activity 4: Design Concepts

Briefly explain the three concepts of design.
Answer:
- Room function: A designer's job is to find out what the function of a room will be: how the room will be used, and who will be using it. A room could be the most beautifully designed space in the world, but if it cannot fulfill all the functions required of that room, the design has failed. For example, one of the main functions of a dining room is eating. When a designer is creating a dining room, he must make sure the room is a convenient place in which to eat. An ideal room is one that provides the most functionality for the owner's lifestyle.
- Mood: Is the client looking for a sleek, modern space or something more casual and warm? A designer must consider the mood a client is trying to express in the room being designed and then use color schemes, furniture, flooring, lighting, and window treatments that are consistent with that mood.
- Harmony: Another guideline that designers must consider is harmony, making sure that all the elements in a room work together to provide function and mood for the client. To ensure harmony, all elements of a design should have a compatible color scheme, a consistent scale, and matching quality. For example, if a designer furnishes a room with high-end leather furniture, she will not want to add an inexpensive plastic coffee table to the design.

Activity 5: Budget

Make a list of design tips to use when working within a budget.

Answer:

Prioritize which rooms, projects, and elements are the most important.

Assess the room for existing furnishings and accessories that can be used in the new design.

Improve, repaint or reinvent uses for existing items instead of replacing them.

Cover imperfections on items instead of replacing them.

Use mirrors to create light and space.

Buy unfinished products and finish them yourself.

Buy secondhand or recycled products.

Save on labor costs by completing the work yourself.

Activity 6: Let's Design a Room!

List the eleven main steps for designing a room.

Answer:

1. Sketch the room
2. Conduct a room audit
3. Draw a floor plan
4. Determine the furniture layout
5. Plan the lighting
6. Choose a color scheme
7. Choose a wall treatment or treatments
8. Choose fabrics
9. Choose furniture
10. Choose window treatments
11. Choose flooring

Activity 7: Step 1: Sketch the Room

What important facts should be included in a sketch of a room?

Answer:

- Length of the room
- Ceiling height
- Breadth of the room
- Height of moldings
- Dimensions of doors and windows
- Distance between windows and doors from the corners and from the ceiling and floor
- Measure any room features such as air conditioner units, built-ins, fireplaces, etc.
- Location of electrical outlets and switches
- Location of lighting fixtures

Activity 8: Step 1: Sketch the Room

Choose a room in your house and pretend you have been hired to design it. Sketch the room.

Answer:

Answers will vary by student.

Activity 9: Step 2: Conduct a Room Audit

Conduct an audit of the room you have chosen to design and record your observations.

Answer:

Answers will vary by student.

Activity 10: Step 3: Draw a Floor Plan

On graph paper, draw a floor plan of the room you have chosen to design. Make sure you note the location of north

Answer:

Answers will vary by student.

Activity 11: Step 4: Determine the Furniture Layout

List and describe the four factors that an interior designer considers when determining furniture layout.

Answer:

1. Balance Lines: To determine the balance lines of the room, you will need to divide the room into four quadrants. Draw two pencil lines across the floor plan to divide the room in half length wise and breadth wise. To keep the room balanced, you will need to have an equal weight of furniture in each quadrant. Your four quadrants do not have to be mirror images of each other; you just want to create a visual balance of furniture.

2. Traffic Patterns: Determine where the traffic patterns will be and mark them on the floor plan to remind you not to put furniture in these places. Many designers recommend leaving 36 inches clear in front of each door opening for the swing of the door and 12 inches clear in front of windows for easy access.

3. Focus: Now is the time to determine what the focus or focal point of the room will be. For example, focal points to consider for a living room or den include fireplaces, home theaters, artwork, and bay windows. Once you have determined the focus of the room, your design will revolve around it.

4. Axis: To establish an axis for the room, draw (to scale) the wall that contains the room's focal point and the wall opposite of the focus. Next, draw a line up the middle of the wall from floor to ceiling through the focus, across the ceiling, and down the opposite wall to the floor. This will help you balance the focus from floor to ceiling. For example, if your focus is a home theater, you will need to put something on the opposite wall of equal visual weight along the axis line.

Activity 12: Step 4: Determine the Furniture Layout

Make 2-3 copies of a floor plan and give each a different furniture layout.

Answer:
Answers will vary by student.

Activity 13: Step 4: Determine the Furniture Layout

In your own words, explain the importance of determining a focus or focal point for a room. Name four things that make good focal points for a living room or den.

Answer:
Answers will vary by student.
Good focal points include fireplaces, home theaters, artwork, and bay windows.

Activity 14: Step 4: Determine the Furniture Layout

Using one of the floor plans you created, establish an axis for the room.

Answer:
Answers will vary by student.

Activity 15: Step 5: Plan the Lighting

Why is lighting important to a room? What should be considered when determining the location of lighting?

Answer:
Lighting helps to make the room functional and it creates a mood.
When determining the location of lighting, make sure to pay attention to where the electrical outlets are situated.

Activity 16: Step 5: Plan the Lighting

Name and describe the two types of lighting used in design.

Answer:
1. Task lighting allows people who use the room to complete tasks such as reading, crafts, and hobbies.
2. Ambient lighting gives sufficient light so people can see where they are going in the room.

Activity 17: Step 6: Choose a Color Scheme

Describe the three main color schemes that designers use.

Answer:
1. Adjacent Schemes: When colors that are used are adjacent to each other on the color wheel, the design is an adjacent color scheme.
2. Complementary Schemes: When colors that are used are opposite each other on the color wheel, the design is a complementary color scheme.
3. Monochromatic Schemes: When a major color is the predominant *and* the accent color, the design is a monochromatic color scheme.

Activity 18: Step 6: Choose a Color Scheme

How do some designers recommend dividing colors in a room?

Answer:

- 60% of a dominant color - walls
- 30% of a secondary color - window treatments and upholstery
- 10% of an accent color - accessories

Activity 19: Step 7: Choose a Wall Treatment

Describe the five principle wall treatments most often used.

Answer:

6. Fabric: Fabric gives added texture to a wall and can produce a rich, warm mood to a room.
7. Mirrors: Mirror treatments allow the designer to make a room look bigger and to increase the amount of light.
8. Natural: Natural materials such as brick, stone, tile, or wood create an earthy mood for the room. Others, such as shells, bamboo, and rattan, can make a room feel light and airy.
9. Paint: Paint is usually the least expensive and most common wall treatment. It is also the most versatile.
10. Wallpaper: Wallpaper, which is usually a plastic or plastic coated paper, is available in solid colors, patterns, and even full wall murals.

Activity 20: Step 8: Choose Fabrics

Create a chart showing some of the advantages and disadvantages of ten common types of fabrics used in design.

Answer:

Fabric Type	Advantages	Disadvantages
Acrylic fabric	Strong, durable, resists insects, mildew and weathering; wrinkle resistant	Generates static electricity, does not absorb moisture, can be uncomfortable
Cotton	Tough material, withstands wear, breathes well, dries quickly	Has a tendency to wrinkle
Glass fabric	Flame resistant, resists insects, mildew, sun damage, and water	Has a tendency to crack
Hemp	Extremely strong and durable, hypo-allergenic, breathes well, resists mildew, absorbs moisture	Wrinkles easily, may be scratchy unless blended with a softer fiber, is not colorfast

Linen	Durable, retains its shape, resists bacteria, dirt, and stains; is naturally lint-free	Wrinkles easily, not as durable as cotton and wool, hard to dye
Nylon	Strongest of all fabrics, easy to dye, repels mildew and moths, washable, dries quickly	Shiny appearance, slippery, flammable, easily damaged by the sun
Polyester	Flame resistant, strong, resists dirt, mildew, and moths; washable	Does not dye well, fades in sunlight
Rayon	Inexpensive alternative to silk, easy to dye	Not very strong, subject to mildew, rots in sunlight
Silk	Luxurious, soft, strong, dyes beautifully	Hard to clean, fades easily
Wool	Tough, durable, soft, luxurious, dyes easily	Delicate, expensive

Activity 21: Step 9: Choose Furniture

Make a list of questions you should ask when choosing furniture.

Answer:

- Does the cost meet the budget?
- Will the piece function in the room?
- Choose an overall style
- Does it match the mood and style of the design?
- Is the piece harmonious with other pieces in the room?
- Is the piece the right size for the space?

Activity 22: Step 10: Choose Window Treatments

Briefly explain the relationship between window treatments and function, mood, and harmony.

Answer:

- Function: Window treatments not only need to make the room look appealing, they must function the way they are needed to; window treatments are often used to provide privacy, control sunlight, control temperature, and control sound.
- Mood: The window treatments you select must fit the mood you are trying to create with the rest of the design. For example, if you are designing a warm, comfortable, earthy mood, you will want to select a window treatment such as bamboos or other natural materials to match that mood - not neon green plastic mini blinds!
- Harmony: Just like other design options, the window treatments should be harmonious with the rest of the design. Consider the quality and scale of the window treatment compared to the rest of the elements you are placing in the room.

Activity 23: Step 11: Choose Flooring

Give examples from the two groups of flooring.

Answer:

Hard flooring treatments include wood, stone, tile, and resilient flooring.
Soft flooring treatments include carpeting and rugs.

Activity 24: Career Opportunities

What are four areas that would fall under specialized design?

Answer:

➢ Product design or product representation

➢ A specific focus on certain design elements such as lighting, kitchen and bath, and closet designs

➢ An exclusive type of client such as geriatric facilities

➢ A particular design style such ergonomic or environmental (green) design

Activity 25: Career Opportunities

What is the difference between an interior decorator and an interior designer?

Answer:

Interior Decorator: An interior decorator is a person who applies the finishing touches to a room or design such as the wall coverings, fabric, furnishings, and accessories. There are certification and continuing education courses for this; however, certification is not required to be an interior decorator.

Interior Designer: An interior designer is responsible for researching the function, mood, and harmony of a space and using specialized knowledge to plan, prepare, and design the space to fit the health, safety, and wellbeing of the client. Interior designers must have a working knowledge of color theory, space planning, building codes, and plumbing and mechanical basics. This profession requires a degree from an accredited institution and a license.

Made in the USA
Middletown, DE
09 July 2023